AN EVENT-BASED SCIENCE MODULE

FRAUD!

TEACHER'S GUIDE

Russell G. Wright

P9-DCI-977

DALE SEYMOUR PUBLICATIONS®

Parsippany, New Jersey

The developers of Event-Based Science have been encouraged and supported at every step in the creative process by the superintendent and board of education of Montgomery County Public Schools, Rockville, Maryland (MCPS). The superintendent and board are committed to the systemic improvement of science instruction, grades preK–12. EBS is one of many projects undertaken to ensure the scientific literacy of all students.

The developers of *Fraud!* pay special tribute to the editors, publisher, and reporters of *USA Today* and NBC News. Without their cooperation and support, the creation of this module would not have been possible.

Student photographs by Janie Tutterow

Executive Editor: Catherine Anderson
Senior Editor: Jeri Hayes
Project Editor: Laura Marshall Alavosus
Production/Manufacturing Director: Janet Yearian
Production/Manufacturing Manager: Karen Edmonds
Senior Production/Manufacturing Coordinator: Roxanne Knoll
Design Director: Jim O'Shea
Design Manager: Jeff Kelly
Text and Cover Design: Frank Loose Design
Cover Photograph: Eyewire.com

This book is published by Dale Seymour Publications®, an imprint of Pearson Learning.

This material is based on work supported by the National Science Foundation under grant number ESI-9550498. Any opinions, findings, conclusions, or recommendations expressed in this publication are those of the Event-Based Science Project and do not necessarily reflect the views of the National Science Foundation.

Printed in the United States of America.

ISBN 0-7690-0031-2
DS29822

1 2 3 4 5 6 7 8 9 10-ML-03 02 01 00 99

This product is printed on recycled paper

Contents

Preface

The Event-Based Science Model

Fraud! is a module covering chemistry concepts related to paints, pigments, and other art materials. It follows the Event-Based Science Instructional Model shown below. All Event-Based Science modules begin by having students watch television coverage of a real event from science, and read *USA Today* and other newspaper reports about it. We call this first step the "hook," because it catches students and holds their interest just as a hook catches and holds a fish. Discussion of the event reveals your students' prior knowledge of the related science concepts. An authentic task creates a need for teams of students to refine their knowledge and explore new concepts and processes. Student demands for needed information are met with hands-on instructional activities that prepare them to complete the task. Interdisciplinary activities found in the back of the module should be completed in the classrooms of teachers from other appropriate disciplines. The task leads to a final product that allows students to apply the science they have learned and to be assessed on the *quality* of their work.

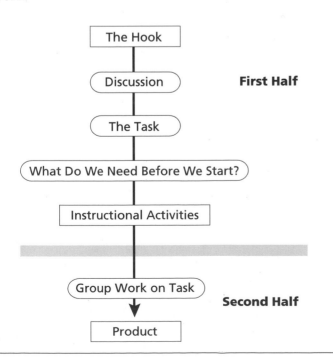

```
          The Hook
             |
         Discussion          First Half
             |
          The Task
             |
   What Do We Need Before We Start?
             |
     Instructional Activities
             |
      Group Work on Task
             |                Second Half
          Product
```

Scientific Literacy

Today, literate citizens must know how to analyze problems, ask critical questions, evaluate competing claims, and formulate and test tentative explanations of events. They also need to acquire scientific knowledge and apply it to new situations. The Event-Based Science model allows students to accomplish all this by placing the study of science in a meaningful and interdisciplinary context in which students see the role that science plays in the lives of ordinary people.

Knowledge can neither be transferred from the mind of the teacher nor from the pages of a textbook. This view of learning leads us to a new paradigm of instruction, one in which students are the workers, the product is knowledge, and teachers are coaches, guides, and advisors assisting students as they construct and test their knowledge. The Event-Based Science model is a constructivist model. It is based on the idea that students will come to know science best if they have been actively engaged in it. Assessment in this paradigm consists of students exhibiting their knowledge through projects, reports, essays and problem solving.

Student Resources

An Event-Based Science module includes a broad range of activities and strategies. Cooperative learning structures, open-ended laboratory investigations, guided discussions, statistical analysis, and performance assessments are included. Have your students conduct all activities found in *Fraud!*

Interdisciplinary activities are set in the context of fraud in the art world, but were written by teachers from mathematics, English, and social studies, to meet the objectives of their disciplines. These interdisciplinary activities are designed to be used by teachers in the other departments of your school. If your school is not organized in a way that facilitates coordination of topics between departments, you may wish to use interdisciplinary activities in your own classroom with appropriate expert teams.

The Event-Based Science module is unlike other textbooks. It tells a story about a real event and contains newspaper articles about the event, interviews with the people involved, and features that explain the scientific concepts involved. However, the collection of resources found here is not meant to be viewed as exhaustive. You may use all of the tricks of the science teaching trade, supplementing the words and activities of the text with your own insights, experiences, explanations, and demonstrations.

Be careful not to succumb to the natural desire to preteach. Save your augmentation of the module for the discussions that will naturally follow EBS activities. Then, when all EBS activities have been completed, and students are busy working on the task, encourage them to find information from sources other than you. Other textbooks, encyclopedias, pamphlets, magazine and newspaper articles, maps, and atlases are all fair game in their search. Have your students take full advantage of Internet, World Wide Web, CD-ROM and other information-age technologies. You may even use a Web browser to link to the Event-Based Science home page—a page established to link you and your students to the world of information about art and chemistry. You will find our home page at: http://www.eventbasedscience.com

The Demand for Change

Writers for the Event-Based Science Project were mindful of the following parameters as they selected the event and developed the task and activities for this unit:

- *National Science Education Standards,* developed by the National Research Council

- *Science for All Americans and Benchmarks for Science Literacy,* developed by the American Association for the Advancement of Science

- research that shows the benefits of assessing students' preconceptions about science; employing a variety of instructional strategies, especially interdisciplinary instruction; and, demonstrating the relevance of science to all people in all cultures

- technologies that have the potential to enormously increase the efficiency and effectiveness of instruction (laser disks, CD-ROM, and the Internet);

- the joy in the search, without which science is dull.

The shape of science education for the twenty-first century is beginning to emerge. The Event-Based Science Project is leading the way.

We hope you enjoy your experience with this unit as much as we did developing it.
—Russell G. Wright, Ed.D.
Project Director and Principal Author

Science Outcomes

Science is a creative process by which people attempt to discover and explain events and objects of the universe. Scientists construct their explanations by observing, questioning, experimenting, and validating. Confirmed discoveries may demand a radical shift in the way we explain an event or object; at other times discoveries merely confirm current explanations or provide evidence for slight modifications of current explanations. Science demands that we question all things; it rejects the labeling of statements as unalterable and it opens itself to continual scrutiny and modification.

The science outcomes listed throughout this document are firmly grounded in a definition of science as both process and product. To communicate the value of this concept of science and to ensure its inclusion in all science classrooms, the Event-Based Science Project has adopted six outcomes that equally and together define the essential science curriculum.

As you read each activity in this teacher's guide, you will find it helpful to refer to the chart that follows. This chart not only defines each outcome, it also specifies typical indicators of mastery of that outcome. Remember, these indicators are only samples of those appropriate for midlevel students.

These six outcomes, known as the Maryland Science Outcomes Model, were developed by a team of Maryland science educators, to be closely aligned with *Science for All Americans* (AAAS, 1989). The outcomes used in EBS materials also match well with the five dimensions of learning outlined in *A Different Kind of Classroom: Teaching with Dimensions of Learning* (Marzano, 1992), published by the Association for Supervision and Curriculum Development (ASCD). Finally, the National Research Council has identified in *National Science Education Standards* (1996), six domains of their Science Content Standards: Unifying Concepts and Processes of Science, Science as Inquiry, Science Subject Matter, Science and Technology, Science in Personal and Social Perspectives, and History and Nature of Science. We believe that if your students master the outcomes listed in this Event-Based Science module, they will have mastered the *National Science Education Standards* as well.

Outcome	Learning Dimension	Sample Indicators
Outcome 1: Students will demonstrate their acquisition and integration of major concepts and unifying themes from the physical sciences.	Concepts of Science	
Outcome 2: Students will demonstrate the ability to interpret and explain information generated by their exploration of scientific phenomena.	Nature of Science	• Design a scientifically valid experiment. • Accept peer review. • Demonstrate that predictions are based on data.
Outcome 3: Students will demonstrate ways of thinking and acting inherent in the practice of science.	Habits of Mind	• Modify ideas based on new evidence. • Demand evidence supporting claims. • Ask questions in order to clarify.
Outcome 4: Students will demonstrate positive attitudes toward science and its relevance to the individual, society, and the environment, and demonstrate confidence in their ability to practice science.	Attitudes	• Demonstrate belief in one's ability to understand science. • Explore the role of science in science and nonscience careers.

Outcome 5: Students will demonstrate the ability to employ the language, instruments, methods, and materials of science for collecting, organizing, interpreting, and communicating information.	Processes of Science	• Use developmentally appropriate instruments and materials to demonstrate:
		  ➤ controlling variables
		  ➤ conducting an experiment
		  ➤ using statistics for analysis
		• Communicate procedures and findings.

Outcome 6: Students will demonstrate the ability to apply science in solving problems and making personal decisions about issues affecting the individual, society, and the environment.	Applications of Science	• Use knowledge of science to solve authentic problems and/or to take a position relative to an issue.

Introduction

This Event-Based Science module uses an interview with master art forger David Stein, and the story of the exquisite, Vermeer-like forgeries of Han van Meegeren to establish the context for a *six-week* study of chemistry. Unlike traditional curricula, an Event-Based Science Module provides a student-centered, interdisciplinary, inquiry-oriented, program that emphasizes cooperative learning, teamwork, independent research, hands-on investigations, and exploration of authentic tasks. The event-based approach encourages students to develop habits of mind common to scientists, and gives a self-differentiating structure in which every student can be challenged and succeed.

If your students have never paid attention to the interactions of matter around them, chemistry may seem as abstract to them as the study of black holes and quasars. We have selected an art fraud as the entry into the study of chemistry in order to increase the interest of adolescents in what is often seen by them as an irrelevant and dry topic.

THE HOOK: An *NBC News* interview with infamous art forger David Stein provides the hook for *Fraud!* Small-group discussion of the answers to guiding questions allows the teacher to uncover students' prior knowledge about chemistry.

THE MASK: This unit really begins when you have your students make a mask. Although best completed in art class, the design and construction of a mask is important to this unit. Devote a day or two of science class time if necessary.

THE TASK: While making and learning about masks in their art class, in your class, your students will become the newest employees of a laboratory that is competing for a contract with the famous art auction house Sotheby's. Before they can compete, your students must prepare themselves. Students will complete a series of science activities in which they test various items to determine their physical and chemical properties. Following each activity, a class discussion will result in a "protocol," or agreed-upon procedure for the tests used in that activity. Discussions will also include the usefulness of each test in determining authenticity.

Performance assessment is embedded within all activities and within the task itself. In addition, performance assessment items are included for those who feel compelled to "test" at the end of units, marking periods, or semesters.

After the class is divided into five-member laboratory teams, each team should meet to develop a list of questions they wish to have answered before they are ready to start. Science Activities and Discovery Files are designed to provide the background information that will answer their science-related questions. Interdisciplinary Activities provide additional information.

Once the actual task begins, it is the teachers job to provide sealed plastic bags containing test materials and a biography of the artist who used those materials to construct a mask. You should also assist as necessary.

As the task progresses, it may be necessary to hold short expert-group working sessions. That way, experts can help each other with particularly sticky parts of the task. Most of each class period during the task will be spent by teams working together. Once the task begins, there will be little time for whole-class instruction.

The culminating event for this unit is a report on the authenticity of the materials in a bag from Sotheby's.

Six-Week Timeline for Presenting This Unit

Week 1	Hook and Task Introduction	Mask Construction	Rusty Elements
Week 2	Rusty Elements	Earn Your pH, Dee	
Week 3	Fiber Space	Metal of Honor	
Week 4	What a Mass!		
Week 5	Students Work on the Task		
Week 6		Presentation and Evaluation	

The Hook

The hook used to generate interest in chemistry is an *NBC News* interview with infamous art forger David Stein. Small-group discussion of the answers to guiding questions allows the teacher to uncover students' prior knowledge of chemistry.

Before showing the videotape, divide your class into the four-member teams that will be working together on the task. Students will stay in these teams throughout the module, so assign them carefully. Examine the requirements of the task (see Student Edition, pages 4–5) as a guide to assigning students to groups.

Play the videotaped news coverage for your class. After viewing, each student-team should work with one other team. They should discuss what they have seen and answer the five discussion questions below. Designate a recorder for each double team. The recorder will write the group's best answer to each question on a large sheet of newsprint for use in a Blackboard Share session. Also designate a reporter. In Blackboard Share, the reporter's job is to report the team's answers using the recorded list.

After all double teams have reported their answers, the class should look for areas where they see agreement and/or disagreement. The sheets of newsprint can be saved and used at the end of the unit as a way for students to compare what they knew about chemistry at the beginning of the unit with what they know at the end of the unit.

Discussion Questions

1. In the past, when you tried to copy the work of a famous artist, why didn't your copy look real?

2. What could you do to make a copy more like an original?

3. The colored matter in paint is called a *pigment*. Paint pigments are usually chemical compounds. What are compounds, and how are they different from elements?

4. Pigments sometimes are man-made and sometimes they are found in nature. Natural pigments can come from rocks or plants. Some plant pigments change color when the pH changes. What is pH?

5. Metals can be used to decorate works of art. What are some characteristics of metals that you can use to tell one metal from another?

THE STORY—PART 1

Collaboration with the Enemy

In September 1939, the world was shaken. The German army invaded Poland and Czechoslovakia. Their appetite for conquest unsatisfied, they pushed forward. In 1940, Holland fell.

As you might imagine, people don't like it when their country is invaded by another country. The Dutch were no exception. Besides fighting back, they tried desperately to protect their national treasures. And among their most valued treasures were paintings by such Dutch masters as Rembrandt, Vermeer, and Van Gogh.

As the Dutch people feared, Nazi officers were very interested in these valued works of art. One of the most infamous Nazi officers was Hermann Goering. He was a Nazi leader, chief of the German air force, and lover of fine art. He bought and seized artworks all over Europe.

Vermeer's paintings were of special interest to Goering. Although it dates from the 1600s, Vermeer's work was highly valued in 1940. So shortly after the German occupation of Holland, General Goering bought a famous Vermeer. He got it from a little-known Dutch painter named Han van Meegeren. Collaborating with the enemy they called it, but van Meegeren was well paid.

van Meegeren, Christ and the Adultress, Dienst Verspreide Rijkscollecties

In May 1945 an army of liberation moved quickly across Europe. World War II was ending. Within days of the liberation of Holland, Dutch police stood on van Meegeren's doorstep. The "Vermeer" in General Goering's collection had been linked to van Meegeren. The police were there to arrest him—the charge, treason.

Then van Meegeren sat in a prison cell for six weeks before he finally confessed. But van Meegeren did not confess to collaborating with the enemy; he confessed to defrauding the enemy.

He explained that the "Vermeer" he sold Goering was not a Vermeer at all. It was a fraud! He—van Meegeren—had actually painted it. What Goering thought was a genuine Vermeer called *Christ and the Adulteress*, was actually a fake.

The police did not believe van Meegeren's story. They demanded that he paint a new forgery to prove he could do such work. It took him two weeks but van Meegeren was able to paint a reasonable Vermeer imitation. This new painting was used as evidence in his trial a year later.

STUDENT VOICES

I prefer sculpting. A good sculpture comes to life. I like its three-dimensional quality.

In fifth grade, we were doing art as a group, and a few days later another group of kids copied our work. They just changed it around a little bit, but it made me kind of mad. It was our work they were copying.

DARREN RIVAS
FAYETTEVILLE, GA

The Story—Part 1   1

The Task

After showing and discussing the Hook, this unit really begins when your students design and construct a mask. Have your students complete their masks in art class if possible. If not, spend a day or two letting them create the masks in your class. Follow the instructions for the mask interdisciplinary activity.

Materials used to decorate the masks will be the same kinds of materials tested during the science activities, and the same kinds of materials tested at the conclusion.

Have your students present their masks to the class and explain the rituals and customs surrounding their mask design. Display the masks around your classroom.

Students will now become the new employees of a laboratory. They will complete a series of science activities in which they test various items to determine the physical and chemical properties. Following each activity, hold a class discussion. What should be the "protocol" for the tests used in that activity? Which tests will be useful in determining authenticity? You may help your students as they struggle with these issues; but don't deny them the satisfaction that results from successfully meeting a challenge.

INS lab: The real thing in finding fakes

Center combats surge in use of counterfeit IDs

By Maria Puente
USA TODAY

McLEAN, Va. — The museum of fakes has no sign on the door and no telephone listing in tourist brochures.

It is tucked away near a giant shopping mall in a suite of offices in a suburb of Washington, D.C. And it's one of the Immigration and Naturalization Service's best weapons to fight illegal immigration.

The museum, officially the Forensic Document Laboratory, has the USA's largest collection of fake birth certificates, Social Security cards, passports and resident alien cards, commonly called green cards.

Specialists at the lab use the latest technology to distinguish genuine documents from fakes. "In prosecuting higher-level criminals, our people are the ones who put the nail in the coffin by providing the expert testimony," says James Hesse, an intelligence specialist.

Separating authentic documents from counterfeit documents is increasingly critical to the INS's campaign to shut down counterfeiters who supply fake documents to illegal immigrants. This lab has become even more crucial as Congress prepares to pass legislation establishing projects to study methods of verifying identification of people applying for jobs.

Illegal immigrants use fake documents to get jobs and social services benefits that they're not entitled to. Some economists say this costs taxpayers billions a year.

Counterfeiting is a booming and lucrative business:

► One operation broken up last May in Los Angeles netted more than $1 million a month in sales of Social Security cards, green cards and driver's licenses that sold for $120 to $180 each.

► Last month, INS agents arrested six people in Washington, D.C., and charged them with running a counterfeiting operation that produced about 1,000 fake green cards a year.

► In November, agents seized 79,000 phony driver's licenses, green cards and Social Security cards worth an estimated $7 million in a raid on a family-run Los Angeles ring.

Counterfeit documents for the domestic market are usually of poorer quality than those used internationally. An illegal immigrant in the United States needs only to fool an untrained employer. Someone trying to get into the country must slip by a trained INS agent.

International smugglers may charge illegal immigrants $15,000 to $30,000 for a high-quality U.S. passport or green card and transport to the USA.

In 1993, the INS lab handled 2,788 counterfeiting cases. By the end of this year, the caseload is expected to grow to about 4,000, a 44% increase.

A major problem with counterfeiting is that "if you can print it, someone can fake it," Hesse says.

Six specialists who work in the lab are experts on handwriting analysis, fingerprinting technology and the growth of new counterfeiting methods. They help train INS officers and other government and law enforcement officers in the U.S. and worldwide in the art of detecting fakes.

At the INS lab, each specialist is responsible for a different region of the world. Handwriting experts learn signatures of officials in countries who are authorized to issue documents.

Besides the huge collection of fakes, the lab has thousands of genuine documents from 3,100 U.S. counties, 50 states and 220 countries.

A recent addition to the collection is a special Olympics visa. It will be issued by the State Department to about 40,000 foreign athletes, coaches, trainers, judges, Olympic Committee officials and journalists expected in Atlanta this summer for the 1996 Games.

Lab officials already have sent out bulletins to U.S. ports-of-entry explaining how real Olympic visas will look and giving tips on detecting fakes.

Counterfeiters have access to state-of-the-art printing technology. But INS experts have equally advanced technology. For example, Haitian passports include a latent image that can be seen only under certain lighting and is hard for counterfeiters to reproduce.

Other countries also get help from the lab. Some are installing the "photo-phone," which transmits crystal-clear images over phone lines. It allows border guards to send pictures of suspicious documents to the lab for instant examination.

But sometimes low-tech equipment is all that's needed to nail a counterfeiter.

Take the case of a man who put his own picture on someone else's passport. The lab detected that a barely visible seal was misaligned. Preparing for trial, the lab blew up a photo of the doctored passport, then attached a movable arrow to show clearly the misalignment. "He pleaded guilty right after he saw that photo," Hesse says.

Document cases

The number of fake-document cases handled by the Immigration and Naturalization Service's Forensic Document Laboratory is rising steadily.

Year	Cases
1993	2,788
1994	3,126
1995	3,358
1996	*2,300

* First seven months of 1996; 4,000 are projected by the end of the year
Source: Immigration and Naturalization Service

USA TODAY, 8 MAY, 1996

Picasso portrait nets $29 million

By Christine Sparta
USA TODAY

NEW YORK — A rare portrait from Picasso's blue period sold Monday for more than $29 million — three times its estimated value and the most a painting has brought in at auction in five years.

"We're delighted with the sale," says Matthew Weigman, Sotheby's spokesman.

The high price is considered an indication the art market — in a slump since 1990 — might be heating up.

Another sign: the $14.85 million sale of The Hindu Pose by Henri Matisse, best price ever for a Matisse sold at auction.

Bidding for Picasso's Angel Fernandez de Soto, also called The Absinthe Drinker, began at $8 million and rose until a phone bid went unanswered.

Including commission, the anonymous private collector paid $29,152,500.

The 1903 portrait of Picasso's friend in a Barcelona cafe sold for $22,000 in 1946.

The last major Picasso auctioned was Yo Picasso, which sold for $47.9 million in 1989.

USA TODAY, 9 MAY, 1995

ART FRAUD CASE: Lucio Ambroselli of Loomis, Calif., was charged with art fraud after collecting $410,000 from State Farm insurance on two Italian Renaissance paintings he reported stolen — although the artworks have been hanging in the Vatican for centuries. An appraiser at Ambroselli's home had seen only photos of the paintings attached to crates that Ambroselli, 57, said held the paintings.

USA TODAY, 14 SEPTEMBER, 1995

2   *Fraud!*

Fraud in the Auction House?

An art auction is about to begin. The auctioneer pounds the gavel. The crowd grows quiet and the auctioneer says, "I offer for bid, item number FSW-430-1 on your program. We have verified that this painting is a genuine Chagall. It and all other works being auctioned today will include a letter of authenticity."

"Do I hear one hundred thirty-five thousand dollars for this beautiful Chagall?"

An original painting is not only a work of art, it can also be an investment. This painting was checked by the auction house . . . they were sure it was real.

But what if they're wrong? What if it isn't real? What if it's a fraud?

Art fraud is a serious crime. Using sophisticated techniques, criminals create fake works of art. An art fraud can be a painting or limited-edition print, a statue, a vase, or a prehistoric artifact. Art forgeries are made to appear as if they are the work of a famous artist or ancient artisan.

The forger hopes to sell a fake for thousands or hundreds of thousands of dollars. One investor spent $35,000 on Salvador Dali graphics and later found out that the collection was worth only the price of the paper on which they were printed—almost nothing! Art fraud is a $100 million-a-year business.

In 1991, a warehouse in Long Island was found to contain almost 73,000 works of art. Supposedly by Dali, Miro, Picasso, and Chagall, they were all fakes! Today, when someone is about to spend thousands of dollars on a piece of art, they need proof that the work is real. This is where you come into the picture.

The Charge

You and your classmates are newly hired laboratory technicians. You have just started working for a company that specializes in identifying unknown substances. Your company has a reputation for thorough and accurate analysis of all materials brought to it. If a statue is supposed to come from an area that does not have any copper, but your laboratory finds copper in the statue, perhaps the statue is not

Chagall, Self-Portrait, Philadelphia Museum of Art

genuine after all. Or, if your laboratory finds pigments in a painting by Chagall that he didn't know about or have access to, it's probably also a fake!

Sotheby's of New York and London is one of the leading auction houses in the world. For over 250 years, they have been offering art at auction. No matter what your interest—photography or folk art, Swiss watches or French wine, furniture or paintings, books or baseball cards—you can find it being auctioned at Sotheby's.

Sotheby's is considering using your laboratory to help them determine the authenticity of art objects they will be offering for auction. However, they want to make sure you really are as good as people say you are. They have sent a collection of mask materials for you to analyze. These are not all from ancient masks. Some of these masks were made by modern-day artists using ordinary materials—paper, metals, fibers, inks, etc. Sotheby's knows exactly what the artists used. They want to see if you can identify the materials and relate them to an artist.

In the science activity *What a Mass!* for example, students will learn about density and develop a protocol for testing the density of pieces of metal that some of them used to decorate their masks. They may decide, however, that unless the pieces of metal are large enough, their technique for determining density lacks the precision necessary to distinguish one metal from another.

Although this unit requires students to perform lots of measurements, it's not a good idea to review the units of measurement or techniques of measurement before beginning. Instead, deal with measurement issues as they arise.

Be sure to have reference booklets available in class. Physical science texts or other references should be easily accessible. Although a periodic table of the elements appears in the Student Edition of *Fraud!*, a large periodic table of the elements should be posted in your classroom. A *CRC* manual may help students find physical constants, however, it may be difficult for most students to use and understand.

Students are asked to devise standard procedures for testing materials. Trial-and-error method will probably follow brainstorming. Check with groups from time to time to assess the applicability of their methods. Don't interfere with the natural discovery process by telling groups what to do. The activities may take longer this way, but more learning will take place.

Groups should keep daily notes and develop a reference booklet to contain everything they've written. Stress the importance of keeping everything so that mistakes can be traced back to their sources. Notes can be sloppy in their original formats, but should be rewritten and modified as warranted.

Mini-Activity: Writing a Protocol

Event-Based Science modules promote science learning through trial-and-error and discovery. This is fine for the learning part, but for the true application of science, standard procedures are needed. Students will use trial-and-error and discovery to solve basic problems that will lead them to standard testing procedures (protocols). They will be expected to use these protocols to test various materials.

Try the activity below to guide your students to an understanding of protocols. Have students bring in boxes (only) from foods that have multistep preparation directions. Be sure that groups have several different kinds of foods. Give task teams three minutes to list all similarities. The primary similarities should be that all boxes list standard ingredients, nutrition facts, and directions. Choose two boxes of the same items and have two students read the package directions in unison. Ask the class if these seem to be standard directions for that product. Then ask if persons who live in Maine and California would get the same results if they followed the recipe exactly.

Modify one of the steps of the recipe by either overcooking, or eliminating or substituting ingredients. Ask if the results might be positive or negative?

Lead a discussion on the need for standard procedures in conducting tests. Tell students that a scientist has just figured out how to make something work and wants to share it. What might she do?

Explain to students that one thing that makes science unique is that scientists have to be able to replicate (reproduce) each other's research and get the same results. Therefore, they need a clear set of directions to give to each other.

Give students a Lab Report Guide and Statement of Authenticity (see Blackline Masters, page 39 and 40) and review them. The lab report may be modified. However, Part 1 is the standard report. Compare it to a recipe or box directions. Explain that the actual steps for carrying out scientific tests, like the ones they are doing, are called *protocols*. Students must record the class-selected protocol for each science activity.

The Final Test

After all activities and protocols have been completed, your students are ready for the final test. Each team will receive a bag from Sotheby's. Each bag will contain materials—supposedly taken from a mask—and a biography of the artist who created it. The team's job is to use their testing protocols to determine the authenticity of the materials.

Bags must be set up by you. Each bag should contain a black piece of yarn (either natural or synthetic), a piece of metal foil, a piece of chromatography paper with a black line drawn across it, and a small square of aluminum foil folded to contain a powder—sand, baking soda, salt, or sugar.

How to set up each bag. You will need to create a bag for each team. Photocopy enough of the Artist Biographies (see Blackline Masters, pages 36-38) so that each team will get one. Place an artist's biography in each bag. Bags can either contain items that are a perfect match for the description on the biography of the artist, they can contain a total mismatch, or something in between. Although bags representing true frauds would probably only be off by one item, you should tailor each bag to the skill level of the team that will receive the bag. (A team whose members are working hard but struggling with this unit should have more than one chance to catch a mismatch. A highly skilled team might have a very subtle clue, or no mismatches at all.)

Note: If you plan to use the Performance Assessment for this module, you should only use Biographies 1–4 for the final part of the task. Save Biography 5 for everyone to use as they complete the performance assessment.

And don't forget to keep a record of the items you place in each bag. This record will be your answer key.

Science Activities

Rusty Elements

Purpose
To investigate the differences among elements, compounds, and mixtures.

Background
You and the other laboratory technicians are excited about the chance that your company might win the contract from Sotheby's. But the lab director is right. A few weeks of training and practice are needed. During this time, you and the other new lab technicians will explore the properties of various substances and come up with a protocol—or procedure—for testing each one. That way, when the masks arrive, everyone in the lab will be conducting the tests the same way.

According to the agenda, today's training deals with elements, compounds, and mixtures. Written in bold letters across the chalkboard at the front of the room is this statement:

Analyzing any unknown substance begins with the fundamental question: What is it made of?

Tension is high as the director enters. She strides around the room, dangling a broken piece of rusty bicycle chain in front of each technician. When everyone has seen the chain, she finally speaks.

"What is the brown substance covering this chain?" she asks.

"Rust!" All shout, thankful the question is so easy.

"Is rust an *element*, a *compound*, or a *mixture?*" She demands.

Seeing that the room has fallen strangely silent, she turns and leaves.
The training has begun.

Part 1
What is an element? Gold is an element; so are silver and iron. Does that mean that all elements are metals? Is rust an element?

Materials
- Periodic Table of the Elements (page 10)
- Elements List (page 13)
- sand
- iron wool
- iron filings
- candle
- metal tongs
- balance scale

Procedure
Oxygen in the air we breathe is an element; so is the carbon in your pencil lead. Look at the Periodic Table of the Elements on page 10, or the list of Elements on page 13. Do you recognize any of the other elements? Can you find rust there?

List any elements you have heard of before. What do they have in common? If you still don't know what an element is, read the Discovery File, There's Matter In My Paint! on page 9. When you learn the meaning of *element*, write it in your own words. Next, state why you believe that rust is, or is not, an element.

CAUTION: Use goggles for this part.

Pull off a piece of iron wool about 1 cm in diameter. Grip it firmly, using long metal tongs. Hold the ball of iron wool in the flame of a candle and record any changes you notice. Examine the result with a microscope or magnifying lens.

Now pull off another piece of iron wool. Put it in a plastic cup and add some water. Leave it overnight in a cool place. Examine it the next day.

Did the iron wool change? If its surface changed, try to scrape off some of it. Can you think of a way to change these scrapings back into iron wool again? Can it be done by ordinary means? Would you like to try? Write your ideas in the reference booklet you are developing for the Task.

Part 2

Materials (Same as for Part 1)

Procedure
Use a balance scale to determine the mass of about 2 tablespoons of iron filings. Combine the iron with about 2 tablespoons of sand. Mix them together well.

Can the iron and sand be separated? Brainstorm with your group to come up with the most efficient way to separate the two substances. If you want to use any materials that are not listed, ask your teacher. Try to recover all of each substance. The mass of the iron after the separation

Objective
Classify materials as elements, compounds, or mixtures.

Science Outcomes
- Concepts of Science
- Nature of Science
- Habits of Mind
- Attitudes
- Processes of Science
- Applications of Science

Science Concepts
- Elements
- Compounds
- Mixtures
- Atoms

NSES Content Standards

Properties and Changes of Properties in Matter

- A substance has characteristic properties that are independent of the amount of the substance.

- A mixture of substances can often be separated into the original substances using one or more of the characteristic properties.

- Substances react chemically in characteristic ways with other substances to form new substances—com-

will tell you whether or not your method worked.

Part 3

Materials
- 3 black nonpermanent markers (each marker should be a different brand and have its own identifying label)
- chromatography paper
- plastic cups
- water
- scissors
- metric ruler

Procedure

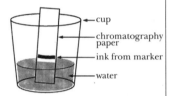

cup
chromatography paper
ink from marker
water

Cut 3 strips of chromatography paper to a length of about 10 cm. With one of the markers, draw a line across the strip at about the halfway point. Put a couple teaspoons of water in a plastic cup. Suspend a strip so that the end of the chromatography paper strip touches the water. Make sure that you design a method that does not allow the paper to fall into the water. Observe what happens as the water moves up the strip.

Repeat this procedure for the remaining markers. Carefully and completely record your results and add them to your reference booklet along with the dried strips of chromatography paper.

Conclusion

Create a data table that organizes what you learned about elements, mixtures, and compounds. You will need space in the table to answer all the questions below.

1. What happened to the iron wool you burned? What happened to the iron wool you soaked in water? What is the chemical name for rust? (Fe_2O_3)

2. Classify the iron wool as *element, compound,* or *mixture.* Give a good reason for your answer.

3. Classify the rust as *element, compound,* or *mixture.* Give a good reason for your answer.

4. Classify the sand and iron filings together as *element, compound,* or *mixture.* Give a good reason for your answer.

5. Classify the marker ink as *element, compound,* or *mixture.* Give a good reason for your answer.

What procedure do you plan to follow to determine whether a substance on the mask is an element, a compound, or a mixture? List the steps of your procedure in your reference booklet.

pounds—with different properties.

- Substances are often placed in categories or groups if they react in similar ways.

- There are more than 100 known elements that combine in different ways to produce compounds.

Description

This is a multipart science activity about matter. Students will work together in teams or pairs to differentiate among elements, compounds, and mixtures. As you know, elements are substances composed of only one type of atom. Compounds contain two or more elements chemically joined by the interaction of their outermost electrons. A compound has properties that are very different from the properties of its components. Mixtures are also combinations of substances, but unlike compounds, the substances in a mixture are not chemically joined, and they keep their own characteristics. Also unlike compounds, the components of a mixture can be physically separated.

A periodic table has been provided on page 10 of the Student Edition, but you should also have a large periodic table of the elements on display in your classroom. Students are asked in Part 1 to look at the names of the elements and write those that are familiar to them. This may require the element list on Student Edition page 13. When students burn the piece of steel wool or soak it in water, both tests accomplish the same thing. The result is the compound *iron oxide,* better known as rust.

Note: Steel wool has been referred to as *iron wool* to emphasize the formation of a compound of iron and oxygen. Steel is actually an alloy, or mixture, of iron and small amounts of other elements. For this activity, steel wool behaves as if it were made of the element iron.

In Part 2 students are asked to determine the mass of 2 tablespoons of iron filings, then mix them with 2 tablespoons of sand. Their challenge is to separate the iron from the sand. Someone will probably want to use a magnet, so have magnets handy too. But be sure to have students wrap magnets in paper or plastic to ease the removal of filings from the magnet. If some of your students want to try another method, encourage them to do so.

When students have finished separating the mixture of iron and sand, they will weigh the filings again. Have students record, in their reference booklets, how close they come to the original mass.

Mixtures can be of two types, homogeneous and heterogeneous. In a heterogeneous mixture, the composition and properties are not uniform. Beef stew is an example of a heterogeneous mixture, as is sand in water and dust suspended in air. A homogeneous mixture is one in which the composition and properties of the mixture are uniform throughout. All samples drawn from it are uniform. Examples of homogeneous mixtures include air, sea water, and brass. Solutions are always homogeneous mixtures. Therefore, a heterogeneous mixture cannot be a solution. In this activity students make a mixture of sand and iron filings. Is it a solution?

Part 3 has students working with a different type of mixture. Inks are mixtures. The chemicals that make up ink retain their own individual characteristics. Students will use paper chromatography to separate the inks of each of three different brands of water-soluble (nonpermanent) felt-tip pens. Before you do this activity, number each pen, and be sure that students include the number in their lab reports. (**Note:** It is very important that all similar pens bear the same number, and that these numbers do not change during the course of this module.) Have students compare their results. Different inks have different compounds in them. Each pen should have its own chromatographic "signature." These signatures are very important. The final task for this unit requires students to identify these ink pigments again.

Chromatography is a technique used to analyze and purify chemical mixtures. It is used in environmental monitoring, food processing, forensics, and in the chemical and pharmaceutical industries. The technique takes advantage of the fact that components of a mixture have different rates of solubility in any given solvent. Since the ink is a mixture, its components keep their unique chemical and physical properties. The mixture is placed on a medium that will "draw" water by capillarity. White coffee filters will work, but the colors won't be quite as distinct as with lab-grade chromatography paper. A solvent (water) is added and allowed to travel across the medium through the mixture. The components that are more attracted to the solvent, and less to the paper, will travel farthest. Conversely, components that are more attracted to the paper, and less to the solvent, will travel the shortest distance.

This experiment works best if the drawn line is horizontal, parallel to the surface of the water. A 400 mL beaker, or equivalent paper or plastic cup, with 10–20 mL of water in it works well. The top of the filter paper can be wrapped around the pencil and attached with a small piece of masking tape. With this setup it can take about 15–20 minutes before the capillary action of the water completely separates the pigments in the ink. Make sure students wait long enough for the colors to finish separating before removing the filter paper from the beaker. The filters can be hung up to dry and later placed in the students' reference booklets. When you discuss the protocol for paper chromatography of water-soluble inks, be sure to establish a time standard. That, as well as a standardized distance between the water and ink line, are very important. Ideally, your students will discover this. Don't be too quick to tell them.

Answers to Conclusion Questions

1. Student data tables will contain all the information asked for in the conclusion questions. Formats will vary, but data tables should have references to elements, compounds, and mixtures. They should have descriptions of the oxidation of iron wool by both water and burning methods. The chemical name for rust is *iron oxide.*

2. Iron is an element. The iron wool burned like a sparkler. Pieces of it turned black and some of it sparked up, falling to the tabletop. If allowed to sit, it becomes rusty. The soaked iron wool also rusted, like a bicycle left out in the rain. **Note:** Steel is actually a mixture of iron and carbon. Since steel wool behaves like elemental iron when it oxidizes, call it *iron wool.* If students question you about it, be prepared to explain the process of steel making, so students know what they were dealing with.

3. Rust is a compound called *iron oxide.* Its elements are bound together and cannot be separated by ordinary means. In addition, rust does not have properties of either iron or oxygen.

4. Sand and iron filings are a *mixture.* They can be separated physically by plucking or with a magnet.

5. Ink must be a mixture because of the way it behaves on the chromatography paper. The components separate physically as they are carried along with water.

Scoring Rubric

- Data table is clearly labeled, complete, and neatly laid out. All conclusion questions are answered correctly and contained in the table. Agreed-upon protocols are recorded, and the dried chromatography strips are mounted.
  = 4 points

- Data table is labeled and complete. All conclusion questions are answered. Agreed-upon protocols are recorded and the dried chromatography strips are mounted.
  = 3 points

- Data table is labeled and mostly complete. Answers contain very little detail and may have errors. Protocols may not have been recorded, but the dried chromatography strips are mounted.
  = 2 points

- Data table is incomplete. Answers are missing or illogical. Protocols and dried chromatography strips are probably unavailable.
  = 1 point

Earn Your pH, Dee

Purpose
To create solutions and determine pH.

Background
As you sit in the conference room for the next round of training, Jim and Dee—two of your fellow laboratory technicians—enter and take seats in the row ahead of yours.

The crystals in the beaker on their table look just like rock candy. So Jim picks one up and starts to put it in his mouth. Dee quickly grabs his hand. "Don't you remember what we learned in lab-tech school? Never put anything in your mouth unless you know what it is!" Dee says.

"I do know what it is," says Jim. "It looks just like rock candy."

"Looks can fool you!" Dee replies.

"You're right!" says Jim. "We have a few minutes, let's test the crystals to see if they're sugar."

As you watch them, Jim and Dee quickly set up an experiment. First they fill 2 plastic cups with water. Next they add a packet of sugar to one cup and the unknown crystals to the other. They stir the contents of both cups.

After a few minutes, the cup with the sugar seems to have no sugar left in it. The unknown crystals are still in the other cup, totally unchanged.

"It's a good thing I didn't lick these crystals," said Jim. "They didn't dissolve. No telling what they are. They might even be poisonous!"

At that very moment, the lab director steps into the room and the second round of training begins.

Part A
Materials
- about 300 mL each of warm water and cold water
- plastic cups
- plastic spoon
- timing device
- sand
- salt
- sugar
- stirrer
- goggles
- hot plate (optional)

Procedure
Sugar, sand, and salt are crystals that can look very similar to each other. But do they behave the same in water? Do they dissolve? Does one dissolve faster than the others?

Design an experiment to test sugar, sand, and salt crystals to see which one dissolves fastest. Use cold water first, then try again with warm water to see if that makes a difference. Be sure to record your results, and save the solution that forms from each of the substances. You will need these solutions and a sample of the water for Part B of this activity.

Part B
Background
In Part A you learned that some things dissolve in water and some do not. Whether a substance dissolves in water or not is a property of the substance. Solubility, the ease with which a substance dissolves in water, is one of its *physical properties*. The crystals Jim and Dee were testing did not dissolve in water. Dissolving is a *physical change;* the substance and the water can be separated.

When certain substances dissolve in water, their solutions are *acidic*. Other substances form *basic* solutions. When acidic and basic solutions are mixed together, a chemical change takes place. This change is a *chemical reaction*. Some of these chemical reactions are destructive, while others are very gentle. You have probably seen what happens when baking soda (*base*) is mixed with vinegar (*acid*).

The *pH scale* is used to communicate how acidic or alkaline (basic) a solution is. On this scale, distilled water (which is neither an acid nor a base) has a pH of 7 (neutral). Below 7, a solution is acid. Above 7, a solution is alkaline or basic. Concentrated hydrochloric acid can have a pH of 1. It's so strong that it can dissolve some metals. Concentrated sodium hydroxide ("lye" or drain cleaner) can have a pH of 13. It will dissolve hair and other proteins. Skin is a protein!

You can test liquids using a special paper called pH paper. When dipped in a solution, pH paper has a color related to the pH of the solution. It is then compared to a standard color scale and the matching color indicates pH of the solution.

Objective
Create solutions and test for pH.

Science Outcomes
- Concepts of Science
- Nature of Science
- Habits of Mind
- Attitudes
- Processes of Science

Science Concepts
- Solutions
- Solubility
- Acid
- Base
- pH

NSES Content Standards
Properties and Changes of Properties in Matter
- A substance has characteristic properties, including solubility, that are independent of the amount of the substance.
- Substances react chemically in characteristic ways with other substances to form new substances—compounds—with different properties.
- Substances are often placed in categories or groups if they react in similar ways—acids and bases.

Materials for Part B
- vinegar
- baking soda
- solutions from part A
- a variety of other labeled substances to test, including plain water and distilled water
- pH paper

CAUTION: Wear goggles when working with these materials.

Procedure

Different household substances have their own characteristic pH. Design a table on which to record the pH of several substances, including the solutions from Procedure A. Be sure to have a place on your table where you can record the names of the substances, and another place where you can tell whether each substance is acid, basic, or neutral.

Before you start, you should explore some of the issues and decide what procedure to use. For example, does it matter whether you test a liquid itself or the liquid added to water? Does the pH change if you add more of a substance to the water? How about the temperature of the water? Does that matter?

After you have explored the issues, decided on your procedure, and measured the pH of at least ten solutions, it's time for a little fun.

You can now carry out a simple acid-base reaction. In a sink, mix vinegar solution with baking-soda solution. Add small amounts at first and record your observations. When the reaction

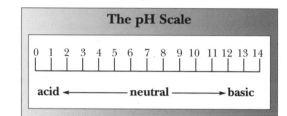

The pH Scale

0 1 2 3 4 5 6 7 8 9 10 11 12 13 14

acid ← neutral → basic

stops, test the pH and record. Repeat until the reaction stops. After each trial, test the pH again.

Conclusion

1. Which substances in Part A dissolved in water and which did not? How did the temperature of the water affect the way the substances dissolved?
2. When you tested the pH of the three solutions from Part A, what did you find?
3. What happened to the pH when you mixed vinegar and baking soda? Why do you think this happened?
4. Can pH be used to test unknown substances? How would you go about it?

Create a colorful visual display showing the various pH readings from your tests. Be sure the pH scale reads 0 to 14. Be creative.

Description

In Part A of this activity, students will work together in pairs to investigate solutes and solvents. A solvent is the substance into which a solute dissolves. The substance being dissolved is the solute. Students will dissolve two solutes—salt and sugar—in the solvent water. They will use sand as a control. Students should notice that salt and sugar dissolve but sand does not. Salt and sugar can form solutions in water; sand cannot.

Be sure to review laboratory safety procedures with your students before letting them use the hot plate. Carefully supervise this stage of the activity.

In Part B, students are introduced to the concept of acids and bases by testing the pH of some common household solutions. Provide some of the following solutions for your students to test: lemon juice, milk, vinegar, crushed grapes, seawater, detergent, soft drinks, ammonia, pure water, and rainwater.

Acids are compounds that contain hydrogen atoms that are released as charged particles, or ions, when the compound is dissolved in water. The term *pH* is used to indicate the concentration of hydrogen ions in solution. Seven is neutral. As pH readings move toward zero, the solution is more acidic. As readings increase to 14, the solution is more basic (alkaline).

The pH number is actually the negative logarithm to the base 10 of the hydrogen-ion concentration in a solution. However, middle school students have no use for this fact—you probably don't either. Your students should simply know that acidic substances taste sour (lemons, oranges), and alkaline substances taste bitter (baking soda, tonic water). Cleaning products are often alkaline.

Strong acids and strong bases are equally harmful. Care should always be used when handling either one. Students should wear goggles while conducting tests on pH.

pH of Common Substances:

lemons	2.3
vinegar	2.9
powdered lemonade	values will vary, but acidic
soft drinks	3.0
grapes	4.0
rainwater	5.7
milk	6.5
pure water	7.0
seawater	8.5
ammonia	11.1

The pH of rainwater will vary depending on the quality of the air in the neighborhood. When fossil fuels are burned, oxides of nitrogen and sulfur are produced and released into the air. These dissolve in water and form nitric acid and sulfuric acid which produce *acid rain.*

After the completing this activity, hold a class discussion about standardized procedures for determining pH. This is the protocol for the final task. Also discuss the usefulness of pH in testing substances that may be found on a mask.

Answers to Conclusion Questions

1. Some substances, such as sugar and salt, dissolve in water; others, like sand, do not. Stirring a mixture and using hot water help to make things dissolve faster.

2. The pH of two of the substances tested in procedure A is the same as plain water. Adding salt and sugar does not change the pH of a solution. Neither salt nor sugar releases hydrogen ions into the solution when they dissolve. Sand may or may not change the pH, depending on minerals present in the sand.

3. The pH of vinegar is acidic; baking soda is alkaline. Mixed together, the pH value tends to move toward neutral. The acid-base reaction stops when one substance or the other runs out. If they both run out at the same time, the resulting solution will have a pH of 7. However, if there is vinegar left, the solution will be somewhat acidic. If there is baking soda left, it will be somewhat basic.

4. The pH scale could be used to test unknown substances. While it would not provide a precise identification of a substance, it could help to rule out some possibilities.

The display should contain samples of pH paper and a key to the scale. It should also have explanations of pH in general, and the pH of the substances they tested.

Scoring Rubric

- Data tables and pH display are clearly labeled, complete, and neatly laid out. Data and pH display are colorful, legible, and easy to read. Answers to questions are well-thought-out, logical, and contain supporting explanations. = 4 points

- Data tables and pH display are labeled and complete. The pH display is colorful. Answers to questions are logical, and contain some supporting explanations. = 3 points

- Data tables and pH display are labeled and almost complete. Answers to questions are logical but may lack supporting explanations. = 2 points

- Data tables and pH display are not complete. Answers are missing or illogical. = 1 points

Objective

Test the physical and chemical properties of fibers.

Science Outcomes

- Concepts of Science
- Nature of Science
- Habits of Mind
- Attitudes
- Processes of Science

Science Concepts

- Physical properties and changes
- Chemical properties and changes
- Man-made and natural fibers

NSES Content Standards

Properties and Changes of Properties in Matter

- A substance has characteristic properties that are independent of the amount of the substance.
- Substances react chemically in characteristic ways with other substances.
- Substances often are placed in categories or groups if they react in similar ways; man-made and natural fibers are examples of two such groups.

Fiber Space

Purpose

To test physical and chemical properties of fibers.

Background

Sam, another technician in your lab, was recently at the hardware store buying a sheet of plywood. When he searched his trunk for something to use to tie the plywood to the roof, he found several different kinds of rope. The pieces of rope had different thicknesses and lengths, and they looked and felt different. He would use one to help him get home. Sam searched his pockets but couldn't find his pocket knife.

A clerk from the hardware store was smoking a cigarette as he watched Sam's predicament. He offered Sam his butane lighter to burn through the ropes. Sam accepted the offer, but he couldn't resist reminding the clerk that smoking causes lung cancer. The clerk said he knew it, but couldn't stop smoking. "Addicted, I guess," he said.

Sam noticed that some ropes burned very quickly, some took much longer to burn, and some "melted." And one of the ropes smelled very bad as it burned.

He pulled on each piece of rope to test it. Some seemed stronger than others. One of them could be pulled apart into smaller strands. Finally, Sam chose one of the ropes, tied the plywood to his car, and drove home.

As he drove, Sam began to think that maybe a burn test would help the lab identify the different fibers in the mask. He wrote his idea on a scrap of paper so he wouldn't forget to tell his team on Monday.

He couldn't wait to see their faces when they burned the stinky one!

Materials

- scissors
- cotton yarn
- wool yarn
- acrylic yarn
- candle
- matches
- microscope or hand lens
- forceps
- sheet of aluminum foil or watchglass

Procedure

Different fibers may not all burn the same. Brainstorm with your group a way to test the "burn properties" of different fibers. Design guidelines for the test and a data table where you can record results.

Fray the ends of each fiber you wish to test. Examine the samples under a microscope and make detailed drawings of them.

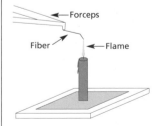

Carefully burn the fibers, keeping track of all observations. You may want to collect other fibers and even hair to test too.

CAUTION: Be careful as you burn the fibers. Hold the burning material WITH FORCEPS as far away from you as you can! Some fibers burn VERY HOT and may DRIP! BE CAREFUL! Make sure that if a drip occurs, the drip will fall on a piece of aluminum foil or other flame-proof surface. If you are using plastic forceps, make sure the flame does not touch the plastic.

Examine burned fibers under a microscope and record any changes you notice.

Make a "Before" and "After" display of your fibers.

Conclusion

1. Your team has examined a ceremonial headpiece supposedly worn by Moses. Your findings suggest it is composed of wood, gold, silver, wool, diamond, and acrylic. Is this one the real thing? Why?

2. The United States Government has regulations concerning the flammability of sleepwear for children. Fabrics must be treated with a flame retardant before they can be used to make sleepwear. Which of the fibers you tested would be the *worst* choice for sleepwear if the standards didn't exist? Explain your reasoning.

Description

CAUTION! It is very important to review laboratory safety procedures with the class before beginning the experiment in this activity. Care should be taken when students work with a heat source such as a candle or Bunsen burner. Goggles must be worn at all times. Students should tie loose hair back. No loose clothing should be worn. The work area should be kept clean and clear of clutter. Review with your students how to safely strike a match or light a burner. Closely monitor all activities involving a flame.

In the activity, students will design and carry out various tests to determine some of the physical and chemical properties of fibers. Have your students explain the procedure they plan to use for burning the fibers before you give them any matches. If necessary, have them write the procedure down before they begin testing on their own. Synthetic fibers burn extremely hot and will melt. Students should use forceps to handle all fibers and make sure the melting synthetics do not drip on them or anything else they might damage. Have ceramic dishes or glass beakers for the fibers to be placed in after burning. Fumes from the burning fibers can be strong. Conduct this activity near an open window or fume hood. Demonstrate to students how to conduct a test for smell by wafting the odor. Hold the substance at a distance and use your hand to move the air toward your nose.

Students will explore the physical and chemical properties of the fibers they are testing. A physical property can be observed or measured without altering the identity of a material. Physical properties can be divided into two types. *Extensive* physical properties depend on the amount of matter present and include concepts such as mass, length, and volume. *Intensive* physical properties do not depend on the amount of matter present. They include such things as density, malleability, color, and melting point. Substances undergoing physical change retain their own characteristic properties. In this activity students will be observing such physical properties as appearance and strength of the fibers.

A chemical *property* refers to the ability of a substance to react with other substances, to undergo changes that alter its identity. A chemical *change* has occurred when new substances with new properties have formed. In this activity students burn fibers. Both the presence of an odor and the release of heat indicates that a chemical change has taken place. The fiber is reacting with oxygen in the air. Burning is always a chemical change. The ability to burn is a chemical property.

Answers To Conclusion Questions

1. It is very unlikely that the headpiece was really worn by Moses. It contains a manmade fiber that was not available at that point in history. This question helps develop the thought processes your students will use when they determine the authenticity of the mask materials at the end of the task.

2. Acrylic would be the worst fabric to use as sleepwear because if there were a fire, the material would become extremely hot and melt onto the skin.

Scoring Rubric

- Fibers are neatly displayed, and clearly labeled. Drawings of fibers are labeled and contain excellent detail. Interesting observations have been recorded. Answers include the question stem and are easy to read, logical, and contain supporting evidence. = 4 points

- Fibers are displayed, and labeled. Drawings of fibers are labeled and contain good detail. Some observations have been recorded. Answers are logical, and contain some supporting evidence. = 3 points

- Fibers are displayed. Drawings of fibers are labeled but lack detail. Observations may not have been recorded. Answers are logical but contain little supporting evidence. = 2 points

- Some fibers are displayed. Drawings of fibers are incomplete or lack labels. Observations have been recorded. Answers are missing or illogical. = 1 point

Objective

Investigate some physical properties of metals.

Science Outcomes

- Concepts of Science
- Nature of Science
- Habits of Mind
- Attitudes
- Processes of Science

Science Concepts

- Physical properties of metals
- Electrical circuits
- Conductors and insulators
- Heat transfer
- Magnetism

NSES Content Standards

Properties and Changes of Properties in Matter

- A substance has characteristic properties that are independent of the amount of the substance.
- Substances are often placed in categories or groups if they react in similar ways; metals is an example of such a group.
- There are more than 100 known elements that combine in different ways to produce compounds.

Metal of Honor

Purpose
To determine conductive and magnetic properties of some metals.

Background
Your laboratory supervisor volunteers as an expert for the *Ask an Expert* site on the World Wide Web. At that site students can get their questions answered by authorities like your supervisor and you. An e-mail from a third-grade teacher has arrived. His students are curious about the properties of metals. They have submitted some of their observations and questions. The teacher wants professionals like you to answer the questions and suggest activities that will demonstrate the answers.

Here are the questions the kids submitted:

Observation #1: My cat chewed through a lamp cord and got shocked. Luckily, the circuit breaker blew and saved the cat's life.

Question: Why don't you get shocked when you touch an electric cord, but you do if you touch the wire inside?

Observation #2: My mom was following a recipe that had her sear some meat. She had a lot of meat, so she used two pans. One was iron and the other was aluminum. She put them on the burner and waited a few minutes. To test the temperature, she put a few drops of water on the aluminum pan. The water instantly danced around, hissed, then evaporated. It took longer for the iron pan to get that hot.

Question: Which metals heat more quickly than other metals?

Observation #3: My dad used to hang my "artwork" on the refrigerator door with these cute little animal magnets. In our new house the refrigerator has wood-paneled doors and the magnets won't stick.

Question: What are some materials that are magnetic?

Keep a detailed log of your findings while you do the following experiments. Remember, the log must answer all the questions students asked and suggest activities they can do to answer the questions for themselves. Be sure to write procedures plainly and provide many diagrams for students to use.

Conductivity
Conductor: Material that allows electrical current or heat to flow through it.

Insulator: Material that doesn't allow electrical current or heat to flow through it.

Part 1
Turning on the Juice

Materials
- 1.5-volt battery

- 3 six-inch wires with bare ends
- water
- salt
- beaker
- flashlight light bulb with holder
- paper clip
- flat pencil eraser
- pencil "lead"
- one strip each of steel, copper, aluminum, and brass

Procedure
Building a circuit tester: To make a circuit tester for testing the conductivity of unknown objects, copy the plan shown in the diagram below.

As a control, test the paper clip and eraser first. Then test all objects to see if they conduct electricity. Test saltwater and see if that conducts electricity.

Part 2
Turning Up the Heat

Materials
- candle
- metal strips
- ring stand and clamp or other support
- timing device
- goggles

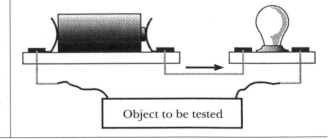

Object to be tested

Transfer of Energy

- Energy is a property of many substances and is associated with heat, light, electricity, etc.

- Heat moves in predictable ways.

- Electrical circuits provide a means of transferring electrical energy.

Description

Electrical Conductivity

In this activity, students perform a variety of tests on metals to determine some of their physical properties.

Closely monitor activities involving electricity and flame. Care should be taken when students work with a heat source such as a candle or Bunsen burner. Safety standards such as goggles at all times, hair tied back, no loose clothing, clean work area, should be employed by all groups. Review with students how to safely strike a match.

Part 1 of the activity has your students building an electric circuit to test electrical conductivity of a variety of objects. Page 28 of the Student Edition has a diagram for constructing the device. Avoid too much instruction. Allow your students to struggle with this until they are successful. However, you should warn students never to run a wire directly from one pole of a battery to the other. It will complete a circuit, but the wire will get very hot.

If the metal strips you use are clean, free of rust, and of similar size, students will find that they all will conduct electricity. They will probably conclude that conductivity of electricity is not a useful test for distinguishing one metal from another. Students will also test an eraser (as a control for nonconductivity), and a solution of saltwater. Students are not told how to mix salt with water to test the solution. Varying concen-trations will give varying results.

If you have an ammeter or multimeter available, have your students measure amperage or resistance and see the differences in conductivity between the different metals.

Additional materials for testing could include: vinegar, baking soda, plastics, paper, iron wool, etc.

Heat Conductivity

Part 2 of this activity involves the conductivity of heat. Although different metals conduct heat differently, there are other variables that can affect the conductivity of metal strips. First it is important to use metal strips of similar size and shape. Placement of the candle flame in relationship to the metal strip is also important. A distance of about 12 cm from the tip of the candle flame to the metal seems to yield more consistent data, as opposed to having the flame touch the metal directly.

This activity asks your students to brainstorm a procedure for testing heat conductivity. A demonstration by you of the different suggestions will help the class decide which one will work best. The best idea we found involves attaching a penny to the underside of the metal strip with a few drops of wax, then placing a candle under the other end of the strip and timing how long before the penny drops.

A ring stand and clamp are in the materials list. Use them to hold the strips as they are tested.

HINTS: Metal strips need to be cooled down between tests. Wax can easily be cleaned off the metal strips with steel wool.

Specific heat is the measure of how much heat is needed to raise the temperature of one gram of a substance by one Celsius degree. The samples with which you are working will not have a constant mass. For instance, your aluminum sample may be lighter than your steel sample. Therefore, the relative degree of heat conductivity the students will discover is true for their samples only.

Remember that the goal of each activity in this module is to give students a means for testing various unknowns in order to authenticate a mask from Sotheby's. It will help if you not only discuss with your class the "protocol" for conducting a test, but also the usefulness of that test. Since all metals conduct electricity, electrical conductivity may not be a useful way of distinguishing one metal from another. Since a difference in heat conductivity may be hard to measure on the small pieces of metal used to decorate a mask, it may also not be of any use.

As your students come to the realization that only the test for magnetism will be of any help to them, have students brainstorm other tests or observations they can perform on the metals that might help them identify them. Some are simple and useful, such as: observe the color and look at them under a microscope; or see how easy it is to scratch them. Others suggestions—like seeing which falls to the ground more quickly—may reveal misconceptions in the minds of your students that should be addressed.

Answers to Conclusion Questions

Explanations of the children's observations include:

Observation 1: Metal wire is a conductor of electricity, the rubber or plastic coating around the wire is an insulator.

Observation 2: Different metals have different rates at which they absorb and transfer heat.

Observation 3: Anything containing iron, steel, or nickel is magnetic. However, nickel coins contain too little nickel to be attracted to a magnet.

1. Metals are not the only conductors of electricity. Solutions with electrolytes are also conductors to varying degrees. Evidence: saltwater will allow for a current flow.

2. Review students' work to get the general trend for this answer. Since there are so many different combinations of metals with different shapes, thicknesses, densities, etc., it is impossible to give a general answer in this manual. Compare from class to class to get an overall picture. A table of physical constants such as ones found in the *CRC Manual* may help you to plot a general trend for the materials you chose. If all students use metals of similar shapes and sizes, they will at least be able to place them in order from best to worst conductor of heat.

3. Again, the answer to this question will have to be deduced by the class using standard procedures with the same materials.

Scoring Rubric

- Student has correct explanations for each of the three child observations, and correct answers to the conclusion questions. The table of metals ranked by conductivity and magnetism is neat, well organized, and clearly communicates its information. If asked, student can produce complete log entries to support answers to questions. = 3 points

- Student has correct explanations for at least two of the child observations, and answers to the conclusion questions. The table of metals ranked by conductivity and magnetism clearly communicates its information. If asked, student can produce some log entries to support answers to questions. = 2 points

- Student has some explanations for at least two of the child observations, and answers to the conclusion questions. The table of metals ranked by conductivity and magnetism is included. If asked, student cannot produce log entries to support answers to questions. = 1 point

What a Mass!

Purpose
To determine the mass and volume relationship for different metals.

Background
All new laboratory technicians learn in lab-tech school that every substance has a constant relationship between its mass and its volume. In fact, this constant is one of the properties of the substance. They also learn that knowing the constant can help them identify an unknown substance.

If only you had tables of those constants, you could use them.

After a search of the lab, no one has been able to find the *CRC Handbook of Chemistry and Physics*. It contains all of the tables and charts anyone could want or need. It even contains the constants for the mass/volume relationships for metals, woods, common liquids, and many other substances.

Time is running out. You need those constants. You have no choice but to develop your own tables. This is going to require very *precise* measurements of mass and volume for all the metals that may be found in the test masks from Sotheby's. That way, constants can be calculated and included in the protocols and procedure manual you are developing.

Materials
- unsharpened pencil
- large metal paper clip
- small metal paper clip
- triple-beam balance
- metric ruler
- 100 mL graduated cylinder
- water
- strips of copper, aluminum, brass, steel

Procedure
For this activity you need three things: the mass of a substance, the volume of the substance,

and the formula for the *mass/volume constant*. The formula is simply the mass divided by the volume.

mass ÷ volume = the constant

The most important thing for you to decide is how to precisely measure the mass and volume. The mass should be no problem if your triple-beam balance is carefully adjusted to zero, and you know how to use it. Volume measurement is a different matter. See the Discovery Files on Volume Control and on Calculating the Constant, page 33.

Conclusion
Record constants for the metals you test in the *Protocols and Procedures* section of the reference booklet your team is developing. Record them in order from the metal with the smallest constant to the one with the largest.

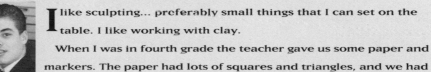

I like sculpting... preferably small things that I can set on the table. I like working with clay.

When I was in fourth grade the teacher gave us some paper and markers. The paper had lots of squares and triangles, and we had to make something out of it. I kept marking each thing the same color, and other kids started copying me. It bothered me at first, but I decided I didn't really care.

NICK GIOVINCO

Objective

To determine the densities of several metal strips.

Science Outcomes

- Concepts of Science

- Nature of Science

- Processes of Science

Science Concepts

- Mass

- Volume

- Density

NSES Content Standards

Properties and Changes of Properties in Matter

- A substance has characteristic properties, such as density, that are independent of the amount of the substance.

Description

This activity is really about density, a very important concept in understanding the properties of matter. However, research has shown that students of all ages have a very difficult time understanding density. The same research has shown that the worst way to teach density is to introduce the word, define it, and then carry out laboratory activities that illustrate it.

With this form of instruction, successful students will be able to define density, but most will be unable to apply the concept to help solve problems.

Therefore, in this activity we refer to the relationship between mass and volume of a substance as a *constant*. Do not mention the word *density* until students reach a point in this activity when they are tired of just saying the word *constant* and are demanding a word to describe the constant.

The conclusion for this activity is in the form of a ranked record of the constants (densities) of the metals tested. The correct order is:

substance	constant (density)
aluminum	2.7 g/cm^3
steel	7.9 g/cm^3
brass	8.6 g/cm^3
copper	8.9 g/cm^3

Scoring Rubric

- Densities are recorded in order from smallest to largest. Aluminum is listed first, copper is last, and most densities are close ($< \pm 1$).
  = 3 points

- Densities are recorded in order from smallest to largest. Aluminum is listed first copper is last, but most densities are not close ($> \pm 2$).
  = 2 points

- Densities may not be recorded in order and they are far from the actual densities listed above ($> \pm 3$).
  = 1 point

Interdisciplinary Activities

Art: Making a Mask

Purpose
To incorporate culture-specific design elements in creating a mask.

Materials (for each person)
an assortment of materials for making and decorating a mask

Materials from the *Fraud!* Task
- markers
- yarns (cotton, wool, and acrylic)
- metal foils (iron, copper, aluminum, brass)

Background
Masks have been used for centuries. They continue to play an important role in the ceremonial and economic life of many cultures. Some design elements are found in many different cultures and areas of the world. Other designs are associated with specific cultures. Use the Discovery File, Masks from Different Cultures, page 6, as a guide to designing your own mask.

Procedure
First, build the foundation for your mask. It can be made from a number of different materials. Some methods will take longer than others but will give you a sturdier mask that is more realistic. Other methods are faster. The slower, sturdier methods include papier mâché and plaster gauze. The faster methods include paper plates and brown paper bags. Your teacher will suggest the one that works best in the time you have.

Before you start to decorate your mask, sketch several possible designs. You may base your designs on those of a specific culture, or you may mix design elements. Remember, masks are three-dimensional sculptures. They are not simply painted faces.

After you have selected the sketch you like best, use tagboard, crushed newspaper, or small pieces of wet plaster cloth to build up the features. Paint and/or colored markers can be used to add detail. Feathers, raffia, beads, etc. can then be added for the final touch.
NOTE: Be sure to include one kind of fiber, one metal foil, and one black marker.

Conclusions
When all masks are finished, display them and discuss the designs. You may also wish to see if people can identify specific cultural characteristic(s) in each mask and the artists may want to explain their choices.

STUDENT VOICES

I've always been fascinated with masks. Anybody can hide behind one and go unnoticed. Movies set in the 1700s with big ballroom galas—Marie Antoinette type—had beautiful masks. I once decided to make a very opulent mask like that. But I couldn't afford anything really grand, so I used cardboard and turquoise felt. Also I selected pieces of sequins that would go together, almost in a gemstone style, and some feathers on the side. So I could wear it, I put pink elastic on it. The pink made it very feminine.

FARISA KHALID
MCDONOUGH, GA

40   *Fraud!*

Objective

To incorporate culture-specific design elements in creating a mask.

Concepts

- Design concepts and elements of different cultures

- Mass and form

Description

Students will read and discuss the information in the Discovery File on page 6 that deals with the masks of the Papuans of New Guinea, Northwest Pacific Coast Native Americans, Africans, and the Hopi People. Any visual aids depicting masks from these cultures should also be displayed in your classroom. Students will then select the cultural design elements they wish to emphasize and include them in their sketches. Students should make several sketches and choose their best one for their masks.

This activity does not require a particular technique for building the structure of the mask. Use technique with which you are most comfortable.

Working individually, students should use their sketches as a guide in creating the finished product.

Scoring Rubric

- Mask is well-designed, makes use of at least one specific cultural design element, and displays good craftsmanship = 3 points

- Mask is well-designed but fails to incorporate any specific cultural design elements. Craftsmanship is acceptable = 2 points

- Mask is poorly designed. Design elements and craftsmanship are unacceptable = 1 point

Math: Please, Turn Down the Volume!

Purpose
To investigate volume in order to determine a good method for finding the volume of irregular geometric solids.

Background
Perimeter is the measure of the distance around a geometric figure. The answer to a perimeter problem is given in *units* (one dimension).

triangle: 3 m, 4 m, 5 m
$$P = s_1 + s_2 + s_3$$
$$P = 3 + 4 + 5$$
$$P = 12$$
12 m

rectangle: 3 km, 5 km
$$P = 2l + 2w$$
$$P = 2(3) + 2(5)$$
$$P = 6 + 10$$
16 km

square: 4 cm
$$P = 4s$$
$$P = 4(4)$$
$$P = 16$$
16 cm

circle: Use 3.14 for π, $r = 3$ cm
$$C = 2\pi r$$
$$C = 2(3.14)(3)$$
$$C = 18.84$$
about 19 cm

Area is the measure of the surface of a geometric figure. The answer to an area problem is given in *square units* (two dimensions).

rectangle: 6 m, 4 m
$$A = lw$$
$$A = 6(4)$$
$$A = 24$$
24 m^2

triangle: 2 cm, 5 cm
$$A = \frac{1}{2}bh$$
$$A = 0.5(2)(5)$$
$$A = 5$$
5 cm^2

circle: Use 3.14 for π, $r = 6$ cm
$$A = \pi r^2$$
$$A = (3.14)(6)(6)$$
$$A = 113.04$$
about 113 cm^2

Volume is the measure of space inside a solid geometric figure. The answer is given in *cubic units* (three dimensions).

rectangular prism: 5 cm, 6 cm, 7 cm
$$V = Bh \ (B = lw)$$
$$V = 5(6)(7)$$
$$V = 210$$
210 cm^3

rectangular pyramid: 5 cm, 6 cm, 7 cm (not slant height)
$$V = \frac{1}{3}Bh$$
$$V = 5(6)(7)/3$$
$$V = 70$$
70 cm^3

Surface area is the sum of the measures of the areas of all *faces* of a geometric figure. The answer to a surface-area problem is given in *square units* (two dimensions).

rectangular prism:
5 cm, 6 cm, 7 cm
$$SA = 2lw + 2lh + 2hw$$
$$SA = 2(5)(6) + 2(5)(7) + 2(7)(6)$$
$$SA = 60 + 70 + 84$$
$$SA = 214$$
214 cm^2

cylinder: Use 3.14 for π, $r = 5$ cm, $h = 10$ cm
$$SA = 2\pi r^2 + 2\pi rh$$
$$SA = 2(3.14)(5)(5) + 2(3.14)(5)(10)$$
$$SA = 157 + 314$$
$$SA = 471$$
471 cm^2

Objective
Investigate volume of regular objects and then determine a good method for finding the volume of irregular objects.

Mathematics Concepts
- Perimeter
- Area
- Surface area
- Volume of regular objects
- Volume of irregular objects

Materials
- Meter sticks or metric rulers
- Graduated cylinders
- Water
- Balance

Description
The purpose of this activity is to teach students several methods for estimating the volume of an irregular object. First review the concepts of perimeter, area, surface area, and volume of regular solids.

Following your review, have students work on the practice problems on page 42. When your students get to Practice Problem 8, they will need another formula. You may want to have your students try to find the formula for the volume of a sphere, or you may wish to give it to them. Either way, the formula is $\frac{4}{3}\pi r^3$.

Answer Key
1. 20 cm
2. 3 m^2
3. 384 cm^2
4. 198 cm^3

5. 350 cm^3
6. 108 cm^3
7. 45 cm^3
8. 4,186.67 dm^3 (for $\pi = 3.14$)

Go over the answers with your students. When you are sure that they fully understand the concept of volume, hold up an irregularly shaped object (a rock or a misshapen blob of clay or modeling dough) and ask them, "How would you find the volume of this object?"

This is a perfect place for the cooperative learning strategy called "Think-Pair-Share." Allow your entire class to have two or three minutes to think about the problem individually and try to come up with an answer. Next, have students work in pairs and tell their ideas to one another. Allow five minutes for this. Then, ask several pairs to share the method they devised for finding the volume of the irregular object.

List all ideas on the chalkboard.

Provide the materials listed above (as well as any other material needed), and challenge your students to test their ideas to determine which of their methods is best. Caution them not to alter the shape of the object in the process!

Listed below are some reasonable methods for determining the volume of an irregular object.

1. Estimation—measure all dimensions of the object, then apply a formula for a similarly shaped regular object.

2. Displacement—place the object in a graduated cylinder or measuring cup that is partially filled with water. The change in volume when the object is added equals the volume of the object. Catching and measuring overflow water works well too.

3. Finding the Mass—this works best with Playdough. First take a new piece of Playdough and carefully construct a regular shape. Measure this regular object that you have made, and use the appropriate formula to calculate its volume. Now use a balance to determine the mass of this new regular-shaped piece and the mass of the irregular one. Use proportions to calculate the volume of the irregular object. If you use this

method with Playdough, ask your students if a similar method could be used with a rock without destroying the irregular rock. (Yes. Fashion a similar rock into a regular shape then repeat the procedure.)

Conclusion Prompt

(Post the following prompt on the chalkboard, or use an overhead projector to project it onto a screen.)

A lab technician from Sotheby's has e-mailed a request for help. She needs to determine the volume and mass of a small nugget of metal that came from an ancient mask. Respond to her in an e-mail in which you list the steps in the method that you think would be best for her to use.

Scoring Rubric

- Answers to the eight questions are all correct, and the e-mail to Sotheby's contains all steps needed to measure the volume of an irregular object. = 3 points

- Answers to at least five of the eight questions are correct, and the e-mail to Sotheby's contains most steps needed to measure the volume of an irregular object. = 2 points

- Answers to fewer than four of the eight questions are correct, and the e-mail to Sotheby's lacks steps needed to approximate the volume of an irregular object. = 1 point

Math: Warm-Up Activities

Purpose
To practice math skills using word problems involving volume.

Procedure
Find answers for the following problems as directed by your teacher:

1. Round each of the following masses to the nearest tenth to determine a reasonable approximation of their average.

   15.74 g   16.85 g
   13.37 g   14.27 g

2. A jeweler's apprentice was asked to leave the measurements of a rectangular box before the end of the day. Instead, he left the areas of the faces of the box and a note explaining that each side was measured in whole centimeters. If the areas were 12, 18, and 24 cm^2, what was the volume of the box?
   If each dimension were doubled, what would be the new volume?

3. A spider fell inside a 300 mL beaker. Every twenty minutes it climbed up the equivalent of 30 mL, but fell 20 mL before recovering. How long did it take it to escape from the beaker?

4. Millie Meetre decided to rent rare artwork rather than buy it. *Art Appreciation Plus* charged $1.00 for day one, $2.00 for day two, $3.00 for day three, and so on. *Enjoy Aesthetic Beauty* charged $.50 the first day and then doubled the previous day's fee for each and every additional day. If she kept the artwork for 10 days, how much more would the more expensive offer be?

5. A chemist has 10 cubic centimeters (cm^3) of a 10% solution. She needs to add enough water to produce an 8% solution. Find the number of cubic centimeters of water that must be added.

6. You discovered that 2 cm^3 of substance A and 4 cm^3 of substance B weighed 4.4 grams while 4 cm^3 of substance A and 2 cm^3 of substance B weighed 5.2 grams. Find the mass of 1 cm^3 of substance A.

7. Six groups used 6 graduated cylinders, all the same size, to weigh 5 mL of iron filings. Their results for the mass of the iron filings were 67.7 g, 67.0 g, 35.4 g, 69.1 g, 68.2 g, and 69.1 g. Only the group that had 35.4 g had the correct mass. Do you think that the other groups forgot to subtract the mass of the graduated cyliner? If so, about what were the masses of the graduated cylinders they used?

8. A wooden cube is painted blue on all faces. If it is cut into 27 smaller regular hexahedra, how many will have paint on three faces? . . . two faces? . . . one face? . . . no faces?

9. Find a relationship between volume and pressure based on the information below.

Volume	Pressure
10	240
20	120
30	80
40	60
50	48

Objective

To practice math skills using word problems involving volume.

Description

These warm-up activities can be used in mathematics classes through the Event-Based Science module *Fraud!* Mathematics teachers can also use them as models to create their own warm up activities to support this module.

Answers

1. 15.7   16.9   13.4   14.3
   avg 15.1 g

2. 72 cm^3, 576 m^3

3. 9 hrs 20 min.

4. It would be $456.50 more!

5. 2.5 cm^3

6. 1 g

7. yes; 32.3 g, 31.6 g, 33.7 g, 32.8 g, 32.7 g

8. 8 will have paint on 3 faces, 12 will have paint on 2 faces, 6 will have paint on 1 face, and 1 will have paint on 0 faces.

9. Their products are always 2400.

Social Studies: Make a Display

Purpose
To design and make an informative display highlighting the culture of a civilization or country.

Background
Sotheby's will soon be holding another auction. This auction will feature artifacts from different civilizations and countries. Sotheby's wants your design firm to create displays highlighting the cultures of the featured countries and civilizations.

Procedure
Brainstorm with the class a list of countries and civilizations you have studied this year or ones you already know something about. Choose a civilization or country from the list.

Research the civilization or country of your choice, and create a display that showcases five of the topics below. Be sure to include brief descriptions of the history or meaning of each. Your descriptions may be written or recorded on tape. You may decide to include the mask you made at the beginning of your science project.

You must cover the first three topics and at least two additional topics from this list:

    art
    customs
    dress
    music
    food
    pets
    money
    jewelry
    agriculture
    anything else you like

Make a map with the location of your country or civilization clearly displayed. Use your imagination. You may make a diorama, include posters, or create handmade, full-sized or miniature artifacts.

Conclusion
Exhibit your display for the class. You will play the role of an auctioneer from Sotheby's. Explain why the culture you choose is interesting in order to persuade the class to buy artifacts from that civilization or country.

Objective

Investigate the culture of a civilization or country.

Social Studies Concepts

• Research Skills

• Cultural aspects of civilizations or cultures

Description

Students will choose from a group of characteristics of countries or civilizations that you have or will be studying. They include:

* art
* customs
* dress
  music
  food
  pets
  money
  jewelry
  agriculture

Starred items must be chosen because they lend themselves easily to the creation of "artifacts." Encourage your students to use a mask design in their display. This will provide a better connection between your exploration of cultures and the work your students are doing in science class.

Using these topics, students will create a display that showcases the items and descriptions of the uses or meanings of each. Descriptions may be written or recorded on tape. They may include the mask they made at the beginning of your science project.

The activity culminates with a presentation. Nonpresenting members of the class will pretend to be auctioneers from Sotheby's. Groups will exhibit their projects and explain why their civilization or country should have its artifacts auctioned.

Scoring Rubric

• The map is complete and the display contains 5 or more items or artifacts that highlight the culture of the selected country or civilization. Explanations are clear and complete, and the presentation is clear and concise and contains all displayed information.
= 4 points

• The map is complete and the display contains only 5 items or artifacts that highlight the culture of the selected country or civilization. Explanations are clear and complete, and the presentation is clear and concise and contains most displayed information.
= 3 points

• The map is fairly complete and the display contains only 3 or 4 items or artifacts that highlight the culture of the selected country or civilization. Explanations are unclear or incomplete, and the presentation is unclear and contains some information.
= 2 points

• The map is not complete and the display contains less than 3 items or artifacts that highlight the culture of the selected country or civilization. Explanations are unclear and incomplete, and the presentation poorly done.
= 1 point

English: Reading and Writing Advertisements

The art world is not the only area in which fraud exists. Unscrupulous people intentionally deceive and mislead the public about a range of issues, from health care and nutrition, to vacation homes and travel tours. Gullible, hopeful, and misinformed consumers sometimes fall prey to quick-fix diets, on which one doesn't have to eat less or exercise more to lose weight. Other people fall for the luxury cruise getaways that do not include airfare but do provide lodging in second-rate motels on Caribbean islands. The best safeguards against becoming a victim of such schemes are to avoid impulsive buying, carefully research the product or service, and deal with reputable companies.

Reputable companies must advertise to inform the public about their products in order to make a profit. And even the most reputable companies use advertising techniques that have been proven to persuade consumers to buy their product or service rather than that of their competitors. These techniques are not usually fraudulent, but they may often imply more than they can actually deliver.

The following are some common techniques used by advertisers:

1. *Testimonials* So-called experts, celebrities, or "just plain folks" praise, use, or are associated with the product. The consumer may assume that because someone more knowledgeable than the ordinary consumer, someone famous, or—conversely—someone just like him or her, uses the product, it must be good. But be warned. Michael Jordan may know athletic shoes, but is he really an expert about hot dogs?

2. *Exaggerated Claims* The product is better, stronger, faster. Than what? Can the degree of difference between two different products really be measured?

3. *Use of Statistics* An ad claims that nine out of ten doctors agree that a particular product is an effective pain reliever. Do you know what doctors were part of the survey? What kind of pain is being relieved? Another ad states authoritatively that one toothpaste makes your teeth 32% whiter. Do you know how the whiteness was measured? What are your teeth whiter than? The use of statistics does not mean that one claim is any more accurate than another unsubstantiated claim.

4. *Hidden Information* Read the fine print—if you can. Automobile dealerships and airlines often offer great deals until you read the fine print and discover other fees, restrictions, or blackout dates that make the offers meaningless.

5. *Slogans and Jingles* "You deserve a break today" and "Just do it" may ring in your ears, but do these words tell you anything about the product? Having a break or accomplishing a goal is not dependent on eating a particular hamburger or wearing a certain brand of shoes.

6. *Appeals to Fear, Vanity, or Popularity* Which ads promise you a safer house, a more attractive look, or more friends? Remember that the advertisers may imply these results with the use of visuals in addition to words.

7. *Get on the bandwagon!* It is important to care for the environment and eat healthier foods, and advertisements may suggest that products are environmentally safe or nutritious. But read the labels before you buy; you may be surprised that some products may have environmentally safer alternatives (cloth diapers, for example, instead of disposables) or may not be nutritious at all! (Less fat does not mean fat-free, especially if you eat more of the product because you think it's nutritious.)

Objectives

1. Read, listen to, and view various media critically, identifying persuasive techniques used by advertisers in print and nonprint ads.
2. Record observations according to an established format, such as a chart or database.
3. Use the writing process (or other creative process, such as radio or television production) to create an ad which uses persuasive techniques.
4. Recognize the potential of ads to mislead and deceive the consumer.

Concepts

- Critical reading, listening, and viewing
- Note-taking
- Use of the writing process, including drafting, conferencing, revision, and editing
- Consumer awareness of truth and fraud in advertising
- Radio and television production (optional)

Description

In this activity (which may include reading, listening, viewing, writing, and radio and television production), students examine how advertisers persuade consumers to

8. *Semantics* The study of semantics is concerned with the meanings associated with words. We may have certain emotional responses to some words more than we do to others. Good persuasive writers use words carefully. Read some real estate ads and use your imagination. Do you see a "handy-man special"? This house could easily be a run-down shack, as could a "charming little cottage near the water." The water could be a leaky basement!

Reading/Viewing Assignment
Over the next day or so, pay particular attention to television, newspaper, or magazine ads. Make a chart on which you list the products being advertised, whether or not you would buy each product based on the ad, and the technique(s) used in the ad to persuade you to purchase the products.

Writing Assignment
Once you have examined a number of advertisements for various products and services, create an ad of your own. You may choose an established brand to advertise or develop an entirely new product or service. You may design an ad for a print or nonprint medium. You may even design the package for your product; this may give more information to the consumer.

Before you begin to create the ad, think about the purpose of the product or service, its ingredients or intended results, and those people who would see your ad and use your product or service. Think about what these people would need to know. This may include cost, guarantees of performance, and visual information. Also think about the techniques you will use to persuade consumers to buy your product or service as opposed to similar ones on the market.

After you write your first draft, consult with a partner who might also be the consumer of your product or service. Your partner should read or listen to your advertisement and respond as an educated consumer would. He or she should tell you if your advertisement is convincing and if you are missing any important information. Then revise your ad as necessary and proofread carefully if you have developed a print advertisement. (You can use the Proofreading Guidesheet on page 49 to edit your ad.) Be sure to think about the visual appearance of your ad, adding drawings, photographs, color, and other eye-catching elements to your design. If you are videotaping your ad, you will also need to consider the setting, props, costumes, and actors who will be delivering your sales pitch.

Present your ad and survey the results. See if your public recognizes the techniques you used and if your ads are considered truthful or fraudulent!

buy their products. They are introduced to and will identify various techniques which may extend beyond providing information and may also mislead or deceive. Students will see that there can be a fine line between truthful and fraudulent practices. They will also create their own ads, in which they determine the techniques that are most effective in promoting a specific product.

In the student book, several persuasive techniques are explained. The teacher may tailor the objectives, assignments, and assessments based on the materials available, other curriculum objectives, and various student ability levels.

Materials

- Print media, such as newspapers and magazines

- Non-print media, such as radio and television ads

- Electronic media, such as computers or radio/television production equipment, as available and appropriate

Assessment

The following are ways in which the teacher may assess student attainment of the first two objectives:

1. The teacher test students by having them identify the persuasive techniques used in various ads selected by the teacher.
2. Students turn in their charts or databases with a display of illustrative ads or present their ads and descriptions of them orally.
3. Through class discussion, students show their understanding of the various techniques.

The second two objectives reflect higher-order thinking skills as students synthesize the information they learned from their analysis of ads and apply the persuasive techniques to an original creation. To evaluate the students' achievement of these objectives, teachers should develop a rubric that accommodates specific curriculum objectives or student ability levels.

A rubric, for example, may include the following areas of evaluation with a scoring system which establishes points for objectives met extensively (3 points), satisfactorily (2 points), or poorly (1 point):

- Advertisement contains basic information about a product – name, ingredients or description of product, purpose, intended results, and cost.

- One or more persuasive techniques are used in the advertisement to attract the consumer.

- Advertisement is visually appealing – colorful, aesthetically arranged, or well produced.

- Mechanics, grammar, and usage are correct as appropriate to the advertisement and student's grade/ability level.

- The development of several drafts, conferences, revision, and editing are evidence of the use of a writing process.

- Correct production techniques are used in the development of a radio or television commercial. (Optional)

Performance Assessment

Writing to Persuade

Purpose

To demonstrate knowledge of simple chemistry concepts and the persuasive writing style in a letter to Sotheby's convincing them that a mask is either authentic or a fake.

Background

Your laboratory is one of two finalists and Sotheby's is having a runoff. To help them choose the lab that gets the contract, they will send each of you one more bag of materials. Again, the materials will be from a mask. You and your partners will test it using the protocols you developed during the unit, compare your results with the biography of the artist, and you will individually write a persuasive letter trying to convince Sotheby's of the rightness of your conclusions.

Materials

- Discovery Files of your choice
- The Reference Book your team developed
- Copy of Peer-Response Form (page 48)
- Proofreading Guidesheet (page 49)

Prompt

As a laboratory technician, you have the job of helping your team test one more bag of mask materials, and carefully recording your findings. Then, on your own, you must write a persuasive letter to the managers of Sotheby's.

Begin with an introduction that gets your readers attention. Describe the tests you performed. State the results and your conclusions. Explain the reasons for your conclusions. Use facts and data from science activities and discovery files to support your statements.

Finally, close with a brief conclusion that sums up your points and tells whom to call if the managers have additional questions.

An exceptional letter:
- Has an attention-getting introduction.
- Clearly states an opinion.
- Gives facts to support the opinion.
- Has a strong conclusion.
- Is relatively error-free and follows the conventions of grammar.

Use the Proofreading Guidesheet on page 49 to edit your letter. Have your peers evaluate and react to your letter using a copy of the Peer-Response Form on page 48.

Questions

1. How do you get your readers' attention?
2. How and where is your opinion stated?
3. What information about tests and procedures for chemical and physical properties do you include? What other information might you include?
4. What data and facts do you use to support your opinion.
5. What other data might you use?
6. How could you improve your conclusion to make it stronger?

Objective

Use knowledge of pH, chromatography, conductivity, and burn characteristics of different fibers to evaluate unknown substances from a "mask." Write a letter to Sotheby's auction house persuading them that the "mask" is either authentic or a fraud.

Science Outcomes

- Concepts of Science
- Applications of Science

Science Concepts

- pH
- Solutions
- Acid
- Base
- Element
- Mixture
- Compound
- Physical properties
- Chemical properties
- Metals
- Conductivity
- Magnetism
- Fire

English/Language Arts Concepts

- Form
- Peer response
- Topic
- Proofreading
- Audience
- Editing
- Purpose
- Persuasion

Description

This writing assignment should be completed by individual students in their English classes. Students may be allowed to use the results of the final task from the science class or they may be given a different package to test. Science teachers should refer to the Scoring Rubric: Science on page 34.

Use the Peer-Response Form (page 32) and the Proofreading Guidesheet (page 33) for peer evaluation groups that will help students proofread, edit, and revise their work.

In addition to providing a writing activity from which English teachers may obtain an assessment of students' progress in persuasive writing, this is an opportunity for the science teacher to evaluate science understanding. English teachers should refer to the Scoring Rubric: Writing to Persuade on page 35 for scoring.

Peer-Response Form

Directions

1. Ask your partners to listen carefully as you read your rough draft aloud.

2. Ask your partners to help you improve your writing by telling you their answers to the questions below.

3. On a sheet of lined paper, jot down notes about what your partners say when you ask them these questions:

   a. What did you like best about my rough draft?

   b. What did you have the hardest time understanding about my rough draft?

   c. What can you suggest that I do to improve my rough draft?

4. Ask your partner to use a pencil to place a check mark near any mechanical, spelling, or grammatical construction about which you are uncertain.

5. Return the papers and check your own. Ask your partner for clarification if you do not understand or agree with the comments on your paper. Jot down notes you want to remember when writing your revision.

Proofreading Guidesheet

1. Have you identified the assigned purpose of the writing assignment? Have you accomplished this purpose?

2. Have you written on the assigned topic?

3. Have you identified the assigned form your writing should take? Have you written accordingly?

4. Have you addressed the assigned audience in your writing?

5. Have you used sentences of different lengths and types to make your writing effective?

6. Have you chosen language carefully so the reader understands what you mean?

7. Have you done the following to make your writing clear for someone else to read?

   • used appropriate capitalization

   • kept pronouns clear

   • kept verb tense consistent

   • used correct spelling

   • used correct punctuation

   • used complete sentences

   • made all subjects and verbs agree

   • organized your ideas into logical paragraphs

Scoring Rubric: Science

3 Points

Student correctly states that the mask materials tested are likely to be from the artist whose biography accompanied the materials or they could not be from that artist. (Results will vary depending on the materials selected by the teacher.) Student describes all tests performed (pH, pigment type, metal type, and fiber type), stating the results from each test and conclusions reached. Facts and data support authenticity claim.

2 Points

Student may or may not correctly identify the authenticity of the mask. Student names the tests performed (pH, pigment type, metal type, and fiber type), stating the results from each test and conclusions reached. One incorrect result prevents full support of the authenticity claim.

1 Point

Student may or may not correctly identify the authenticity of the mask. Student performs only some of the tests required. Results from tests performed may not be correct. One or more incorrect or missing results prevent support of the authenticity claim.

Scoring Rubric: Writing to Persuade

3 Points

- These responses identify a clear position and fully support that position. The information is well-developed with relevant personal and factual information.

- These responses contain numerous specific details that more than adequately support the position.

- The writer establishes an organizational plan that is logically and consistently maintained.

- The writer effectively addresses the needs and characteristics of the audience.

- The writer ethically and effectively uses language choices to influence the audience.

2 Points

- These responses demonstrate that the writer identified a position, but that position may lack total clarity. The writer attempts to support the position, but the information included is inadequate, and irrelevant information may interfere with clarity.

- These responses have details, but the details may be too general or may not sufficiently support the position.

- The writer presents an organizational plan that is minimally maintained.

- The writer attempts to address the needs and characteristics of the audience.

- The writer sometimes uses effective language choices to influence the reader.

- Limited problems with grammar and mechanics do not interfere with meaning.

1 Point

- These responses provide little evidence that the writer understood the prompt and attempted to respond to it. The writer fails to identify a position. Some information is presented although it does not clearly relate to the identified position.

- These responses lack sufficient details.

- A clear organization is not maintained.

- The writer did not address the assigned audience.

- The writer did not use language choices that positively influenced the reader.

- Problems with grammar and mechanics significantly interfere with the effectiveness of the writing.

Biographies

Biography 1

The Tsnamous people created this mask about 1000 B.C. Their artists used iron and brass. And when they traded with their neighbors for copper, they sometimes used that too.

Tsnamous artists frequently used a powdery, alkaline (basic) substance on the inside of their masks. A sample of this substance has been wrapped in foil and included with the other samples. The foil package is not from the mask.

The Tsnamous people grew cotton, corn, and tomatoes. They raised sheep and goats, and kept dogs as pets.

The Tsnamous had access to black pigment types #1 and #3. A sample of a black pigment from their mask has been included. It was extracted from the mask and drawn on a piece of chromatography paper for you to analyze. If this mask turns out to be from this 3000 year old society, it could be one of the most important art and archeological discoveries of the century. How likely is it that this mask is authentic?

Biography 2

Adeline McFerson was an American artist of the early 1800s. This mask was supposedly created by her in 1836. From 1830–1846 McFerson used a limited number of materials that she felt best expressed her feelings.

For metals, McFerson would only use aluminum or brass. She liked making earrings for her masks out of these materials.

McFerson was allergic to wool and would break out in a rash if she touched it. Sometimes she used cotton fibers.

McFerson's favorite black pigments were #2 and #3. A specimen of the black pigment from her mask has been included in your sample bag. It was extracted from the mask and drawn on a piece of chromatography paper for you to analyze.

Occasionally, Ms. McFerson would put tiny iron filings on her masks to give them texture. A sample of a dark-colored grainy substance was found on the mask, and a scraping was taken. This substance was wrapped in foil and included in your sample bag. The foil is not part of the mask.

The Metropolitan Museum of Art is having a show of McFerson's work. They hope to use this mask as part of the show. However, they do not want to buy it unless they are sure it's authentic. How likely is it that this mask was created by Adeline McFerson?

Biography 3

Manual Ortega died two years ago, much to the disappointment of those who knew him and appreciated his art. He was known as a painter but it is rumored that he made one mask before his death. In Ortega's journal he wrote about his plan to make a mask. But, although he wrote extensive notes about what he would, and would not, put on such a mask, he made no sketch of the mask.

Last year, Ortega's daughter came to Sotheby's with a mask she said was made by her father. According to her story, he had kept it hidden in a closet unknown to anyone but her.

An art-collector friend of Ortega's examined the mask and told Sotheby's officials that it looks like the mask Manuel showed him, but he can't be sure. "After all," he said, he had "only seen the mask once."

According to Ortega's journal, the mask was to be made out of brass. He also planned to use wool to remind him of his childhood and the sheep he helped raise.

He planned to coat the inside of the mask with baking soda to keep it free of the smells in the closet. A sample of some powdery substance was present on the inside of the mask. A scraping was made and the substance wrapped in foil and included in your sample bag. The foil is not part of the mask.

Ortega's favorite black pigments were #2 and #3, but occasionally he would use #1. A sample of the black pigment from his mask has been included in your bag. It was extracted from the mask and drawn on a piece of chromatography paper for you to analyze. How likely is it that Ortega really created this mask?

Biography 4

A mask was recently discovered in a small town in northern California. Experts believe that the artist was either Sue Lee or Kenny Sung. Both artists lived in the early 1900s, but used different materials.

Ms. Lee used only aluminum and copper. She despised other metals. She loved the feel of cotton but sometimes also used acrylic yarns and threads.

Ms. Lee was very particular about her black pigments. After years of experimentation and research, she decided to only use pigment #2.

Mr. Sung, on the other hand, used pigments #1 and #3. A sample of the black pigment from this mask has been included in your sample bag. It was extracted from the mask and drawn on a piece of chromatography paper for you to analyze.

Ken Sung used brass and aluminum in his masks, but stayed away from other metals after the death of his cat.

Sung preferred to work with natural fibers. Wool was his favorite because of its availability. At a time when many artists were turning to acrylic fibers, Mr. Sung remained loyal to wool.

Both Lee and Sung shared a unique style of mixing sand with iron filings and using the mixture to give the mask a unique texture that would change color over time as the iron rusts. A grainy substance was found on the mask. A scraping has been wrapped in foil and included in your sample. The foil is not part of the mask.

Biography 5

Max Montgomery is a flamboyant British artist. Controversy arises with every new piece he creates. Montgomery has challenged the art community to prove that his latest work, "Man Behind the Mask," was made by him and not by one of his students.

It is known that Montgomery refuses to work with natural fibers, instead preferring acrylic yarns. He feels that synthetic fibers capture the modern age and the innovative human mind.

When it comes to metals, Montgomery uses pure elements, preferring aluminum and copper. He feels that too many artists use alloys.

Sotheby's has learned a secret about Montgomery that not even his art students know. He sprinkles the inside of each mask with $NaHCO_3$ (sodium bicarbonate), to bring good luck to the wearer. A scraping of a white powdery substance was taken and wrapped in foil. The foil is not part of the mask.

Max feels that of all the black pigments, #2 and #3 are the most powerful. A sample of the black pigment from this mask has been included in your sample. It was extracted from the mask and drawn on a piece of chromatography paper for you to analyze. Are you up for this challenge? How likely is it that Max created this mask?

Double-Check Lab Testing, Inc. Lab Report Guide

Phase 1—Formal Lab Report

Purpose

Materials

Procedure

Data and Observations

Results

Conclusion

Phase 2—Verification

Comparison of Your Report to Other Reports

Phase 3—Revised Report

"Bugs" Worked Out

Additional Needed Materials Are Obtained

New Procedure

New Data and Observations

New Results

New Conclusion

Write a Final Formal Lab Report

DOUBLE-CHECK LAB TESTING, INC.
12562 Question Mark Boulevard
Examination, Idaho 59287

"You Spec 'em, We Check 'em"

Statement of Authenticity

Be it known, that upon thorough testing, the object named below has been discovered and duly verified to be

Object tested _____   Serial # _____

If the object tested has been discovered to be a forgery, the following indicator(s) are proof thereof:

_____

_____

_____

If the tests are inconclusive, that is, no hard evidence can be found that the object is either authentic or a forgery, the following indicator(s) are proof thereof:

_____

_____

_____

Group Leader's Signature _____

Group
Member _____   Group
Member _____

Group
Member _____   Group
Member _____